THE PAGEANT DIRECTOR'S HANDBOOK

A Guide for Beginners and a Handy Tool for Everyone!

Reneé Ruby
Poised Productions, LLC
Pageant Media Services

ISBN 978-0-557-09719-7

TABLE OF CONTENTS:

Many thanks to all my wonderful pageant friends!
I love you Molly, Dawn and Victoria!

Special Thanks & Dedication
To Pam Rogers
With Whom I Had the Greatest Time Co-Directing With,
Even Though it Ended Way Too Soon!
Viva Pageants Galore & More!

To my own beauty queen Alexis, you are the jewel of my life and my greatest accomplishment yet! You make me very proud! To Evan my animation king – I can't wait to see what you come up with next! To DJ my sound & lighting tech, entertainment and load-in/out, couldn't have done it without you! And what the heck was American Idol thinking?

To the Love of My Life
And Reason for Living
Eddie
Thank You for Supporting Us and Our Dreams All These Years, You're the Best Husband a Girl Could Ask For!

Introduction

So, you want to direct a pageant! Great! But do you know how to get started? What things will you need? How to direct the production? There are many things you need to know before starting or even deciding to direct a pageant or other production. For our intent and purposes, we are using pageants as our "production". However, the guidelines, ideas, hints and helps can be applied to any type production or competition. This manual is very carefully arranged and put together to give you the best and most useful information in an organized manner.

We surveyed many long time successful pageant directors and received tips and ideas to include. In the back of this manual you will find a resource index that we have personally used or that was referred to us by another director. These will be mostly pageant specific with the exception of the production companies (lighting, sound, production equipment). Be aware that all the information is as true and accurate as possible.

Testimonials

"Miss Renee', Thanks for such a great pageant! The awards were awesome and it ran so smoothly!"

"Finally! A pageant that starts on time! This Dad says Thanks!"

"I just wanted to send you a short note to tell you what a wonderful pageant you have! Everything was so organized and planned out and all of the contestants were relaxed and having fun!"

"Miss Renee', I have never helped at a pageant where I felt like I didn't even need to be there! I learned so much about organization and prioritizing! Makes me want to start my own production!"

"Thank you so much for making every contestant feel special! It was nice to see everyone getting equal treatment and no 'favorites' were singled out! Your advice was invaluable! Let us know what pageant is next!"

CHAPTER 1: PLANNING

What's In a Name? Everything!

Naming Your Pageant:

The only way to have a truly successful production is to plan, plan, and plan. And of course, the trick is to know what you need to plan! Well for starters, what do you name your production? This seems simple enough, but it actually can be a painstaking process that may take a good part of a day. First of all, come up with more than one name or variations of the name you've chosen or ideal you want to represent. For a festival or community event the name may be easy to come with, in other words "a given". However, other names that you may creatively come up with may not be as easily made. Say for instance that you wanted to have a Miss America©? Well, of course, you can't, That name is registered and trademarked! Well, you would be surprised how many names are actually already taken. Always check with your state's Secretary of State Department. This office is responsible for issuing name registrations. There are also federal agencies that will register and trademark your name federally. All of these will charge a fee for their services, should you decide to lock your name in. However, you do not have to register or trademark your name, and once you begin using it as your own you can consider it copyrighted and utilize the © symbol. Be sure your name is unique, descriptive and is not already owned by someone else. Some directors are very territorial about their names and/or icons or symbols. Be sure yours is original! Say for instance that you saw a pageant named "Pageant Princesses International" and you liked it. What you do not want to do is name your pageant "Pageant Princesses National". That is merely a toke-off of a name already used and not very respectful of the current name-holder, whether the name is registered or not. Now I would like to interject that if your pageant is say, a natural pageant, and theirs is glitz you do have a valid genre difference and could possibly go with it. It is your call but just keep in mind that Golden Rule!

Profit & Non-Profit:

To profit or not to profit? That is the question! It is okay to make money from your pageant! If it were not, there would not be much of a reason to write this manual. There are many considerations to make however in deciding whether to profit from your pageant or to establish a non-profit. First of all, if you want to have a non-profit pageant you will want to set up a non-profit organization. This process is long and can be expensive if you cannot do it yourself. If you can afford an attorney to handle the paperwork, you will come out without a headache! Also, you can always set-up a non-profit that will pay you for your personal time and/or expenses and that of others associated with your organization. As long as it is written out and very specific, it is acceptable. Be aware that all non-profit organizations are legally bound to show anyone that inquires their accounting books. So be sure everything is on the up and up!

Budget:

Once you have your name locked in, you need to decide your budget. In the resource index, you will find a budget worksheet that you can use to calculate your expenses. When you have calculated all your expenses then you will have an idea of what your entry fees will need to be. Normally you will want to figure what the least number of contestants you may have enter and use that number as your starting point for breaking even. We normally set 15 as break-even. Therefore, if our expenses equal $1500, then our entry fee should be around $100 per contestant. Will our contestants pay a $100 entry fee? Well, you also have your admission to figure too. Fifteen contestants will bring at least 15 guests and possibly 30 or more! So, split the difference and say there are 22 guests. Start at about $5 per person = $110 divided by 15 will take your entry fees to $93. Anyways, you can see how complex budgeting can be initially. After you get the hang of it though it is a piece of cake. The resource worksheets will help. Just keep in mind that your figures are only on paper and they are only estimates of what might really happen.

There are several things to take into consideration of your budget: venue, judges, awards, staff, auditor, emcee, audio and more. Everything costs money! Some things could be donated or sold at cost for certain considerations like free advertising and that is great! However, do not get too excited at the thought of freebies, it takes a lot of work to get those. Be prepared to do a lot of footwork, telephone contacting and public relations. If you are not the PR kind of person, then skip the thought and move on to budgeting at full cost.

Awards:

Let's talk about awards. Awards are very important to contestants. After all besides bragging rights, why else would they be there? There is a bigger draw to cash awards than most crowns or trophies, but still, most pageants do not offer cash unless they are a scholarship pageant. It is also very hard to promise cash awards for a first year pageant when you have no idea the number of contestants you may draw. Remember this is a business and you must watch out for the bottom line no matter what. If you cannot risk a loss do not try to produce a pageant. There are no guarantees. In the resources section you will also find an awards worksheet that may be helpful in deciding on awards. When developing your application remember to include a prize list. If you are unsure about some of the prizes such as optional awards then just list the awards as "a nice award" or something of that nature so they know they will receive something.

Venue:

Consider your venue. What does your type of pageant call for in a venue? Some places to consider are schools, convention centers, hotels, performing arts centers, civic centers, etc. You may call the town's Visitor & Convention Bureau or Chamber of Commerce for other ideas. Sometimes if you are planning a large multi-day pageant, the CVB will actually negotiate a deal for you because you will be bringing business into their town.

Judges & Auditing:

Now, for your judges and auditors. Large incorporated pageants such as Miss America© and America's National Teenager© require that their judges do not be compensated. They feel that having uncompensated judges prove that their judges are completely unbiased. They do pay for the judges' accommodations and food while they are there but not their transportation to or from, or for their time. Smaller pageants need to be prepared to compensate their judges for their time. Take into consideration the distance they will have to travel and the meals they may have to cover on the way there and back. You want to try to obtain judges that do not judge regularly in your area and try to avoid judges that direct pageants locally. Start seeking judges well before the pageant date and have them reserved for your date. Sometimes judges you have ready to come have unexpected issues and you will lose one or more at the last minute. In these instances, you may not be able to avoid hiring local judges. Try to choose those you know are respected as judges or directors and/or are approve by their state's Miss America prelim pageant. You are not going to make everyone happy in this situation but be honest with you contestants and let them know you have every confidence that your chosen judges will judge in an unbiased and professional manner. One more thing I would like to mention, that is just a pet peeve of mine. You may want to mention to a judge that may be less experienced that they are representing pageantry and that they should give their utmost respect to the contestants presenting themselves by dressing and acting in a professional manner. They should dress in business attire and keep chitchat to a minimum. Be sure they understand your expectations of them. We type out a "Judge's Guidelines" sheet and insert into their books as a subtle reminder of our expectations. Things like, pay attention to every contestant, from the time they make their first step onto the stage until their exit. Be sure your emcee knows not to proceed to the next contestant until they have received a nod from each judge. They need to take their time and the contestants will appreciate it!

Emcee & Sound:

Your emcee and sound tech should be on the same page. Be sure to create a tech script so the sound tech knows what music to play when. If you do not know how to make your own music there are resources listed in the Resource Guide that will give you some solutions. Be aware they emcee should be paid or possibly given a nice gift if they are donating their time or are the reigning queen. Many times your venue will include a sound person. If the sound tech does a great job, do not hesitate to give them a tip even though they are being compensated by the venue. This lays a foundation for next time you may need them. Also, tip any maintenance people that are great helps. Even an extra $5 is a gesture of appreciation for what can seem like a much-unappreciated job.

Staff:

Next you will want to consider what staff you will need. Do not believe for a second you can handle this all by yourself! You can't. Positions to consider are admission, check-in or registration, interview timer, line-up, stage manager, judge's escort, and general "go-fers". Some venues will provide you with a headset communication system that you can use to run a smooth production. If you do not have the use of that, we have found that just using our cellphone with a head set and text messaging is a great substitute. You never know when you need to give the stage manager some piece of information from the check-in table.

Pageant Structure & Application:

The next thing you need to do is plan your pageant structure and develop an application. Your pageant structure has probably already been settled on from the aspect of your award choices. How many divisions you will have and what to name them, if anything; the optionals offered; and other awards. I can tell you from my own experience that a good application is very important. I cannot tell you how many applications I have received that I immediately threw out due to an abundance of spelling and grammatical mistakes or just because they are too cluttered and confusing. Your application is your first impression with many potential contestants and everyone knows how important first impressions are! Look at other applications, find what you like on each one and incorporate it and make it your own style. And PLEASE do not plagiarize someone else's application! Imitation may be the greatest form of flattery but it can also be irritating if you have put a lot of effort into creating a great application just to have someone else take no time and copy it! Some important things to include: divisions and ages; age rule/grace period; times and date; venue address; web address; what kind of walk is expected; attire requirements; things that are or are not allowed; good sportsmanship rule; score receipt; and liability waiver statement and place for signature. You'll also want to collect pertinent info like parent's name(s); contestant's name and age; date of birth; sponsor(s); mailing address and/or email address; home phone and/or work phone; division entering; optionals entering; and amount enclosed and/or due.

NOTES

CHAPTER 2: PROMOTION

Newspapers:

After planning, promotion is the biggest tool in your production arsenal for directing a successful production. After all, if you do not promote your pageant, how will anyone know you are having one? The first place to hit is your area newspapers. Give them ample advance notice so they can fit in your announcement. Usually three weeks notice is required. Usnpl.com is a great resource for finding all the newspapers in your area.

Mailing Lists:

If this is your first pageant a mailing list may be not be available. If you have friends that are directors, you can always ask if they will share their list with you. But do not be upset if they say "no", a good mailing list is like gold. Instead of asking for the mailing list itself, you may ask them if you give them a quantity of applications stamped, with return address on them, and a box of labels, would they print their mailing labels and send them for you. If they agree, purchase a quantity of labels that will be more than enough and let them keep the extras. Or buy two boxes and tell them they can keep the second box as a Thank You. You could also ask them what kind of ink cartridge their printer takes and go buy them one! Be sure to send your applications well in advance. With money being tight for most people now-a-days most pageant families choose only one pageant a month to participate in; so get your aps out at least one month in advance.

E-Mail:

After a mailing list comes an email list. Seasoned pageant directors have both and utilize them equally for initial contact. Email, being postage and paper free is the preferred contact method. This too is like gold and most directors are not going to want to share. So, you may ask them if they will consider sending an informative email to their list for you. If they agree, remember to thank them in some way other than just saying it. Actions are louder than words. As you start to receive applications and emails, you can begin to build your own lists and later on down the road, you may be able to exchange lists with some directors being equally beneficial.

If someone is sending your information to his or her list, you may not have any say in how the email is sent. But if you are sending out your own emails, you want to be creative, colorful and eye-catching with them. Be sure to include the important info and some teasers that will make them want to visit your webpage or open your application immediately. Do not clutter the email with unimportant images but an eye-catching banner or a picture of the crowns you have decided to award may just clinch the deal! Sending emails every few days, weeks before a pageant is a good idea and every day the week before. Do not spam someone that may not want to receive your email, always be sure to put some sort of contact info that they can use to opt out of your mailing list. One spam complaint to your ISP could mean losing your internet provider. Of course the new standard for most lists is by using the internet-based contact site iContact. Visit their website for more information.

Flyers:

Another great way to promote your event is with flyers. Many retail outlets will allow you to post an informational flyer in their store window or they may even let you leave some applications in a conspicuous location. Be sure to hit all the formalwear stores, dance and gymnastics studios, modeling schools or agencies and hair salons. These are the most likely locations potential contestants will visit.

You will also do well by asking directors of other upcoming pageants if you can leave or pass out your applications at their pageant. Most will happily let you do this and be sure you offer to do the same for them! The best way to get your applications out at another pageant is to put them in the hands of the contestants themselves. Most of the time contestants are too busy stressing over the current pageant to think about picking up an application for another pageant but they will at least stick it in their bag for later if you hand them one. Be sure you have the director's approval; some directors are very territorial and would not approve your passing out applications at their pageant. And believe me; you do not want to make an enemy of another director if you can help it!

Social Networking:

Nowadays you cannot have a production without having a "MySpace", "Facebook" or "Twitter" to go along with it. Using these social networks to promote your production is a great way to contact a more targeted audience. Start with your personal account and use it to create a group, page or space. Get more "friends" by going to other pageant sites and making friend requests.

Internet Webpage:

Last but maybe most importantly is having a webpage. You do not necessarily need an entire site or have to have it professionally done initially but you should have one, somewhere. Tripod and Webs.com seem to be particularly popular. Be sure you know what you are doing or have a friend that does do it for you. Besides an unorganized illegible paper application, I cannot stand to see a poorly designed webpage. It should look like you took the time to make it nice, even if it is only a single page where your contestants can go to download an application. It can be expanded into a site after the pageant by posting photos of the winners and next years' information. As your pageant system grows, it would be beneficial to hire a good webmaster to design and maintain an attractive site. There are many good webmasters out there including myself (RubyImage.com)! (OK, shameless plug there! Other resources are listed in the resource index).

NOTES

CHAPTER 3: PRE-PRODUCTION

By now, you should have you pageant up and going. All the pre-planning is done, awards have arrived or are on the way; and your applications and funds are in. So now what? Now you have to prepare for the production itself. Yes, more planning, planning, planning. Read on.

Line-Up/Numbers:

Once you have all of your applications or emcee sheet (the page you will be placing into the emcee book for the emcee to read) together you need to divide them by division. I like to use an expandable document holder with divided sections and place each application into its section of the folder as they come in. This can save a lot of sorting time later on. Organization here is key. Contestant numbering or line-up can be however you choose to work it: alphabetically, first received last in line, random drawing, by request, etc. Each application should have a place on it where you can print the contestant's assigned number; right hand top is usually best. It is also a good idea to have the contestant's division listed somewhere close to the top too for sorting purposes. Next, you will need to assign those numbers! Some directors like to have each division start with number one and some like to just start from the first contestant (#1) and just keep on going until the last. If you are allowing door entries however, this will not be possible so be sure your divisions all begin at their own time so you can assign numbers as they check –in. This way is much harder and less organized but may be beneficial if you live in an area that may generate walk-in contestants. Once your numbers are printed and cut (we use card paper and scrap-booking scissors that create pretty edges) you need to write the contestant's number on their emcee sheet and on a separate list that can be used for the program if you are having one and as a master contestant sheet for the auditor. Then write the contestant's name on the back of their number. If you have anything else that the contestant will be receiving, you may want to bundle the items together or have them pick the items up at another "station" (such as program book, T-Shirts, opening number outfits, etc). If you are collecting photogenic pictures at check-in you will want to create a list of contestants on mailing labels complete with their contestant number and division – then just peel and stick to the back of the photo and place in the expanding folder, in their division. If you are having talent, you will do the same for music.

Script:

Your script is the second most important part of your production after check-in. The entire balance of your production hinges on a good and correct script. In order to develop a good script you must first create a pageant schedule that outlines how your pageant will run. Go over it with a fine-tooth comb, there is no leeway for error here. Your emcee should know what's going on at all times through the script and your stage manager or line-up person should have a copy of the schedule so they know when to line-up who and for what. Every contestant's emcee sheet should be in the correct order, numbered and in their correct division. A script is just what it sounds like – you need to spell out exactly what you want the emcee to say and when. It is just like writing a play. Your emcee book serves a your master for contestant numbers also.

Music:

You will need, minimally, beauty music. You can purchase music already prepared online or you can create your own to fit a theme. Just use accompaniment music or tracks that do not have someone singing words. You may even want to have drum rolls, fanfares, custom openings, sportswear music, etc. You can make it yourself or you can hire someone to create just what you want (by the way, I can do that for you too. (Second shameless plug!). If you have various music to play be sure your sound technician has the music before it is needed, well marked and a copy of the schedule with the music changes notated for them. An experienced sound technician is used to working from a script or schedule and should not need any intervention from you if you have given them the tools they need. The only exception would be if you had a sudden schedule change, say in talent to give someone time for a costume change or something, then your sound tech needs to be informed as quickly and quietly as possible so your production is still running smoothly.

Scoring Sheets/Judges' Books:

Judges and auditor's score sheets are next. If someone is auditing for you they may provide the judge's and auditor's (emcee announcement) sheets for you. If not, you will need to prepare them yourself. There really is only two ways to layout the judge's sheets: one sheet for each contestant, or one sheet for each division. We found using one sheet per division is a more cost effective and accurate way to go. There are a couple of ways to integrate optionals as well. If you are having an over-all, the judges will need to score each contestant individually usually during line-up – this makes the division score sheet very handy because all numbers for each contestant will be on one sheet. This really makes your auditor's job easier too. If optionals are not a part of any title score you can opt to have one optionals sheet for each division and let the judges decide by group decision or by assigning each judge a separate optional. To accomplish this you only need to notate on each optional sheet the contestant numbers that are participating in that particular option and have the judge(s) circle their choice. If all contestants are participating leave off all the numbers and have the judge write it down. Instruct your judges to write neatly and initial any changes. Parents always have the right to see the score sheets so they need to be on the up and up. IF a parent asks to see the score sheets let them know that all scores will have to be posted for everyone to see including their child's. To keep this possibility from occurring you can put a statement in your waiver that the contestant or parent agrees that all decisions are final and non-contestable. You will also need to consider whether to give out scores to contestants. This is a laborious task postproduction and you may want to consider charging for scores if they want them. Also, be aware that friends and sometimes not-so-much friends will share their scores especially if they feel there might have been a discrepancy. Once your sheets are done the way you want them you need to insert them into judge's books. You should also enclose a Thank You card and the judge's compensation inside the books; so be sure you get ones that have an inside pocket. One for each judge, divided into division sections. The judge's book and emcee book are usually put together the night or day before the pageant. The auditor/emcee sheets are the sheets the auditor writes the winner's numbers and names on for the emcee to read. Once again, these sheets should be scripted out and in the order you want the emcee to read the results. Check and double check your numbers and names, judges only know numbers so be sure the names are correct on the master contestant sheet for the auditor and have someone go behind the auditor to be sure they are right. It is very hard to alleviate issues if your emcee announces the number with the incorrect name.

Documents & Signs:

Once you have your script and schedules completely finished you can focus on other goodies you will need. You NEED signs! Below is a list of signs that you may need to post in various places. Put these up right away while you are setting up for the pageant.

- Check-In/Registration
- Admission
- Dressing Rooms
- Quiet Please
- Turn Off Cellphones
- People's Choice Votes
- Donations/Tickets
- Enter/Exit
- Do Not Enter
- No Men Allowed

It is also a good thing to have schedules posted in the dressing rooms so the contestants know what is going on and when. And do not think your signs have to be boring... make them colorful, delightful and interesting – because you want them to be noticed. Bring masking tape to put X's on the floor. If you have forgotten to put a liability waiver on your application it is highly recommended that you have one at check-in and have each contestant or their parent sign before receiving their number. It is always best to be safer than sorry! Lastly, if your pageant will be an all day affair do yourself and your staff a favor and provide food and/or snacks. If you have a large staff, ask everyone to bring a six-pack of drinks and their favorite snack/finger food!

NOTES

CHAPTER 4: PRODUCTION

And away we go! This is the most complex part of your pageant and the most important (to the contestant). If you have followed the pre-production chapter then you are ready to go and you have made your job much easier and more organized.

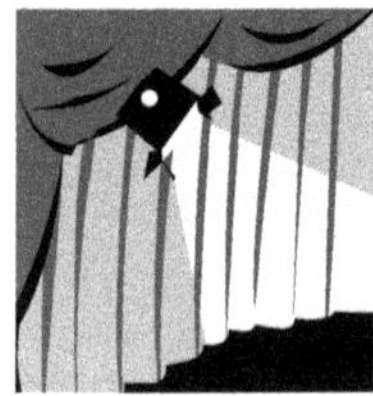

Set-Up:

I know set-up sounds like a pre-production task but normally it is done the morning of or occasionally the day before and really is part of the production. You will need a minimum of four long tables and attractive skirts or table covers on them. The tables are for admission, check-in, judges/auditor and awards. The admission table should be set up in the way of the main entrance. Have a cash box with ample change and a hand stamp and washable inkpad or tickets. If you are collecting money for People's Choice, you will want to do this at the admission table and have a sheet available for the admissions person to write names and amounts on. Be sure you have a person with a strong but sweet personality man this table. They need to be able to stop people at the door to pay admission and not let anyone slip by. If you are charging everyone but contestants admission, the admission person needs to know this and it's a good idea to have it mentioned in your application so there are no surprises and the admission person has something to fall back on. Be sure to post signs on the admission table and on the door entering the venue, so people know they are expected to pay admission as they approach the table. After they have paid admission, contestants should be directed to the check-in table.

The check-in table is where any balances should be paid, photos or documents turned in if you are accepting any at check-in and numbers and paid programs, T-Shirts etc are given out. If you are having a large pageant it would be beneficial to divide check-in into "stations". First a balance or payment station; then the number station where they collect their number; then a t-shirt, program, or other station needed for passing out items to contestants. If you are giving out t-shirts or opening number outfits you need to have a master contestant list and cross out each contestant that picks up a t-shirt. This will keep contestants from receiving duplicate items (by mistake or purposely). If you are having an average to small pageant or the pageant is divided into sessions then one person properly instructed can handle this table. If you have a co-director one of you should man check-in and one should run around making sure everyone knows where things are, setting up the awards table, taking care of the judges, answering questions and overseeing contestant's practice on stage if practice is allowed.

The third table is for the judges. Depending on how many judges you have, you may need more than one table or an extra long one. The auditor can sit at the end of the table or at a separate table. Take into consideration if the auditor will need an electrical outlet, this may determine where they need to sit. Never post your auditor back-stage or in an area out of sight of the audience. Back to the table: place nice decorative items on the table including ample light and hard candy (always have some sugar-free just in case); include a small gift as a special Thank You. This will entice judges to want to judge for you more often and refer other qualified judges to you; and it is just a nice gesture. Be sure there are plenty of working pens and cushions are nice if the pageant is going to be long. We always provide a hot-pink plain sheet of paper in the judge's book. This is the break sheet. If a judge has a personal "issue" they can raise the pink sheet or place it on the table where the emcee can see it and call for a short "judges' intermission". Be sure your emcee is very observant of the judges, especially if you want constructive comments, they need time to write them!

Last but not least you will need an awards table. Your awards table needs to be laid out as the awards will be announced. Optionals awards first, then placement trophies, then the crown and sash (and other awards as applicable) for the winner. Sometimes you can use your awards table as a stage centerpiece, placed in the back with an attractive cover and the awards creatively displayed makes for a nice backdrop. I suggest passing out participation trophies before the emcee announces the winners. Pass them out to everyone and then when the placement trophies are delivered the person giving the awards can pick up the participation trophy and replace it with a placement or winner's trophy. This is the best way to be sure all contestants receive a participation award, so no one goes home empty handed!

You will also need to set up your stage decorations. Ferns, small trees, topiaries, hay bales, arches and draperies all make excellent stage décor. You can rent almost any stage décor from a wedding supply rental place, borrow, buy or make the decorations yourself (see resource index). When deciding on stage décor remember not to clutter your stage and think "professional". Do not place any decorations at the front of the stage that may inhibit a judge's view. Some props you may want to steer away from are balloons, toys or other items that will be distracting to the little ones. I have seen many times a small contestant play with stage props when they should be walking and it had to hurt them in points. Do not forget, everything you put up must come down, so if you have an elaborate stage planned consider the work involved in taking it all down. A pageant is hard work and most times taking down elaborate décor is the last thing you want to think about! If your venue will allow you to come the following day for clean up then by all means take advantage of it!

Another part of setting up is making sure that dressing room lights are on, the air or heat is at a comfortable temperature, trash cans are placed in every corner you can think of, schedules are posted where they need to be, the stage or walking area is clean and free of debris and X's are well marked, your podium/mic is placed where you need it, the judge's room is ready and the bathrooms are clean and well stocked. You may want to also cordon off with tape or rope the rows directly behind the judges so that no one sits behind them and disturbs them or tries to peek over their shoulders. You may also need to cordon an area off for photo and video taking. People can get very annoyed when others keep jumping up or standing through the entire pageant to take photos or video. You want as many people as possible to have an enjoyable pageant experience.

Time to Begin:

Keep an eye on the time; get your judges, emcee, and entertainment (if necessary in place ten minutes before start time. Do not allow contestants to practice on an open stage once the judges are seated. Be sure that someone stays with your judges at all times. It is very important that the production start on time! If something beyond your control happens and you must delay the start time, inform your audience and contestants so they are aware of the issue and are not just sitting around wondering why the production has not begun. If you are having opening number the girls should be lined up or ready to go no later than five minutes before your start time. If no opening number or opening entertainment, have the first division lined-up and ready to go and the next division on stand-by.

Next, lower the house lights and start some music playing ten minutes before start time to let guests know the pageant is about to begin. With everyone in place and a script and schedule to guide the emcee and staff... start your pageant!

Line-Up:

Be sure you have at least one person responsible for line-up; depending on where the dressing rooms are located, two people with walkie-talkies may be necessary. Always have entertainment prepared in case the pageant runs faster than expected and contestants have to change attire and need more time. The person in charge of line-up needs to pay attention to numbers and be sure no one is missing in line-up. Be sure contestants know they will not get a second chance to walk if they miss their place in line-up; they should pay attention to the division calls. The line-up person should also give each and every contestant a once over before they step out on stage. Be sure there are no hang strings hanging our, their tulle layers are smoothed, trains are laid out, hair is in place, etc. This will encourage newer contestants and assure them all that the directors have everyone's best interest in mind. If parents are allowed backstage, be available to help them if necessary and be prepared to "shush" them when the get excited and loud. The line-up person should also be sure contestants do not leave after walking if there is a group line-up. This includes leading the very little ones on stage and showing them exactly where you need them to stand and then to come back and lead them off.

Awards:

If this is your first or debut production, you may not have reigning queens to help hand out awards and crown winners. You may round up some visiting royalty to help or you may do it yourself. Be sure the emcee knows to give the awards person time to give out the award they just announced before moving on to the next award. It's not a race, it's a formal presentation and should be run as such. Have the awards person place participation trophies on the floor in front of every contestant first. Then replace participation trophies with placement ones where necessary. If the winners need to stay for photos the emcee needs to announce this before and after awards presentation. Be sure the judges are escorted to their vehicles or back to the judge's room before concluding the pageant. Thank everyone for attending.

NOTES

CHAPTER 5: POST PRODUCTION

Once your pageant is over you can take a deep breath, and step into postproduction! This is where everything is cleaned up and loose ends are tied.

Clean-Up:

Get right into clean up as soon as possible; try to avoid personal conversation with contestants or their parents other than good wishes and congratulations. Put photogenic photos on the check-in table for contestants to pick up or have someone at the check-in table to hand them out. If someone approaches you for anything other than "thank you, we had a good time" let them know they can contact you in 48 hours with their comments or concerns. Give yourself a day to relax and unwind before allowing yourself to get right into the midst of drama. Do not answer the phone and let contestants know that you will be unavailable the next day. If there are any concerns, the contestant or parent will have time to think it through too before approaching you in an offensive or aggressive manner. If you are personally attacked no matter what, be solid and let them know their behavior is inappropriate and ask them to leave. Let them know you will be happy to address their concerns calmly in a day or so. Sometimes no matter what you do someone will attack you verbally. It is rare but it does happen. If you conduct yourself as nicely and professionally as possible and address the situation at your earliest convenience you have done all that you can. There is normally at least one person who will, and wants to, cause problems.

Bring large plastic bins to carry materials back home in. When cleaning up you can just dump everything in them and then go through them to organize later. Go through the auditorium, dressing rooms, back stage and bathrooms and collect trash and abandoned or forgotten items. Even if you pay a cleaning fee you will be more readily welcomed back if you pick up after yourself. Turn off unnecessary lights, close doors and do whatever else the venue's contract requires of you. Conduct a thorough walk-through just before you leave to catch anything you may have forgotten. Lock the doors behind you if necessary.

Funds:

You most likely will have wads of cash and possibly some checks to deal with when you get home. You should sit down somewhere comfortable and count out the cash and add the checks. Fill out deposit slips for checks and/or any cash you need to deposit to cover any leftover expenses making sure all your expenses are reimbursed before paying yourself or other staff. Some staff you will probably pay out of the cash box before you leave; make a notation of the payment at that time and place in the box so the funds are accounted for. Be sure you take out the money you used for change if you covered it with personal money. If you are holding another production in the near future you may want to hold over funds to seed the next production. If you have paid any staff or judges with checks ensure you let those checks clear before depleting or closing the account. If you are donating proceeds to charity deposit all funds into your account and write out one check once everything has cleared. Be sure to keep a copy of the check for your records or anyone who may ask. If you are sending winner's checks for awards be sure they know you are waiting until all accounts clear before awarding them. This needs to be told to them up-front.

Scores:

If you agree to give contestants their scores, decide up front how you want to handle it. You can have them provide you with a stamped addressed envelope, pay an extra fee to cover your time & postage, email them or give them over the phone. I prefer to email scores and tell contestants they should give me two weeks to get them out before calling me for them.

Thank-You's:

Send thank you notes! Anyone that helped whether compensated or not should receive a thank you note or at the very least a quick phone call to let them know their help was appreciated. You can even do these in advance and mail them the next day after the pageant.

Accolades:

Your winners deserve accolades! A great director will go the extra mile and submit announcements and photos to local area newspapers. This can most likely be done from the comfort of your home or office via email. If you have a website, post their names and photos on the site, create a message board banner; email an announcement to an email list. The more your winners are congratulated publicly the more potential contestants you will get.

Handling Mistakes, Mishaps and Mischief-Makers:

It would be wonderful if every pageant went perfectly and every contestant and guest had nothing but good things to say. In a perfect world maybe. However, here in the real world, nothing is perfect and there is always a mischief-maker in the crowd to try to ruin things! You also may run into some moral or unsportsmanlike issues that need to be dealt with. Below is a working list of common issues and suggestions on how to handle them.

Mistake:

We cannot all be perfect, even judges and auditors make mistakes. Being prepared in the beginning and having a double-checker can prevent most of those issues, but invariably you will find yourself at some point with skewed scores from an auditing mistake that could not be caught or from a disreputable judge. Most of the time this is something you discover later, at home, while going through everything. How you handle that kind of mistake may be a moral issue with you or it may even be the answer to a less than favorable result within one or more divisions. First determine if the error results in a change of optional winners, line-up or winners. Depending on your answer you may decide to make the mistake known and fix it or decide that it is just one of those unfortunate things and make changes to be sure it does not happen again. If the issue is with a particular judge you should make sure you never hire that particular judge again. Confronting the judge is not normally a good idea, you will only face denial or defensiveness and it is just not worth the drama.

Mishaps:

What happens if a contestant falls off the stage? A bit of an extreme example but it has happened, many times! When something happens that may result in physical injury or even extreme embarrassment, the first thing is to stay calm. There must be someone with a cool head to assess the situation and do something about it. If the contestant has not been injured and/or refuses medical treatment then allow them a "do-over" if they would like one. Sometimes things happen beyond one's control and that should not be counted against them. If there is an injury, be sure that quick medical treatment is given and an ambulance is summoned if necessary. This is also why you have your liability waivers. Get the production back up and running as quickly as possible and let guests know that everything is okay and being taken care of. If an ambulance is called, be sure to let guests know that it is only as a precaution.

Other common mishaps have to do with power outages, fire alarms, sound equipment failure, judge's late arrival, contestants' apparel malfunctions and other production mishaps. In these cases you will need to make quick problem-solving decisions. Be sure the audience and the contestants are aware of the issue and that you are working hard to fix it. It is also a good idea for your entertainment to have extra pieces prepared.

As an example, I will never forget halfway through a national pageant production we had three, yes three, contestants in the same division whose zippers malfunctioned! Moms and I ran to the dressing room to see what could be done and the production manager had entertainment standing by. One contestant was cut out of her fashion-wear so she could get into her gown, one contestant's zipper was able to be fixed and another was creatively covered by using around 60 safety pins and the lacing from another contestant's fashion wear to create a lace-up back! And it all took no more than 10 minutes and were ready for their gown competition before the entertainment had to be used! True story!

Mischief Makers:

If you are going to direct competitions, you need to have a thick skin! There are always those who thrive on drama and controversy. These people can make more mischief than the boy who cried wolf! Most of the time you should just ignore them. Let them have their drama and move on. In some instances it is better to nip it in the bud. Confrontations are never easy but sometimes are called for. This will only make you stronger as a director and people will respect you more than if you let the situation run you down. Always approach these issues in a pleasant but firm manner. Let the contestant or guardian say their peace and be sure they know you are listening. Then take the issue head on! Stand firm and be able to back up your statements. Always do this in private unless the other party forces you to make a stand in public. As embarrassingly hard as it is – just do it!

There are literally hundreds of scenarios that mischief-makers can pursue. And there are as many books out there on how to handle controversies. If you can't stand the heat...

Preplanning for next year:

Already? Oh, yes! The earlier the better. Sit down and come up with tentative date(s) and venues and get them reserved. Start a "pageant calendar" to remind yourself of certain tasks in advance. As I am sure you have already discovered preparation is everything and organization is key.

On that note, congratulations on a successful production and best wishes on all the rest yet to come! If you have found this manual useful and want to share your success story please email me and let me know!

Resource Index

NOTES:

EBay
ebay.com or express.ebay.com

Tony's Trophies
tonystrophies.com

Crown Awards
crownawards.com

AB Creations Embroidery – April Bong
abcreationsembroidery.com

Trophy Central
trophycentral.com

Oriental Trading
orientaltrading.com

Banners Plus
pageantsbanners.com

Rainbows End
rainbowsend.com

CD Designs
cdwebdesigns.net

Flaunty Crowns
flauntycreations.com

Tiara Connection
tiaraconnection.com

Wholesale Rhinestone Jewelry
rhinestonejewelry.com

Crystal Crown
crystalcrown.com

Allen's Crowns
acrowns.com

Crown Chic
crownchic.com

Dollar Days Wholesale (bulk)
dollardays.com

NOTES

RESOURCE DOCUMENTS

SAMPLE PAGEANT BUDGET WORK SHEET

Expenses:

Venue:		$
Crowns:		$
Sashes:		$
Trophies:		$
Other Awards:		$
Judges:		$
Emcee/Auditor:		$
Staff:		$
Office Supplies:		$
Postage:		$
Sound/Lighting:		$
Decorating:		$
Other:		$
TOTAL:		$

Income:

Entry Fees:		$
Optionals:		$
Admission:		$
People's Choice:		$
TOTAL:		$

Application Sample:

Name of Production

Date, Time & Place

Age Divisions

Competitions & Fees

(Policies :)

Contestant Requirements: Married, unmarried, without children, appearances require or not, open/closed, etc.
List of Awards: if unsure about some awards like optionals then list as just "award" or "prize" or gift instead of specifying something you may not actually get.
Attire and appearance instructions: glitz, natural, in-between, pageant wear, Sunday best, etc
Explanation of any optionals or titles that are not self-explanatory
Rules of conduct
Contact Info: Director's names', phone, mailing address, payment info

Division:
Contestant Name: Age: DOB:
Parent Name:
Address:
City: State: Zip:
Email Address:

Liability Waiver: release from harm director, volunteers, staff and/or venue from theft or injury and judges decisions are final....
Signature: Date:

Judges' Scoresheets:

By Contestant: harder to audit but easier on judges, deters comparison of one contestant to another, uses much more paper… interview, beauty, casual wear etc all go on separate sheets…

PAGEANT NAME

Contestant's Number:
Division:____________

INTERVIEW
1-10 Each

Appearance	Personality	General Knowledge	Communication Skills

BEAUTY
1-10 Each

Poise/Modeling	Stage Presence	Personality	Attire

________WEAR

1-10 Each

Poise/Modeling	Stage Presence	Personality	Attire

OPTIONALS (1-10)

Facial Beauty:
Photogenic:

Etc

JUDGE INITIAL: ______________

INTERVIEW SCORESHEET
MISS

SCORING SCALE 1 – 10 ON EACH

#	APPEAR ANCE	PERSONA LITY	GENERAL KNOWLED GE	CONVERS ATION SKILLS	COMMENTS

SPORTSWEAR
JUNIOR - TEEN – MISS
SCORE 1 – 10

#	OVERALL APPEARANCE	MODELING	INTRODUCTION	COMMENTS

JUDGE INITIAL: ________________

SAMPLES

ON-STAGE PRESENTATION
(EVENING GOWN)

JUNIOR – TEEN – MISS

SCORE 1-10

#	OVERALL APPEARANCE	POISE MODELING	STAGE PRESENCE	COMMENTS

JUDGE INITIAL: ______________

CHOOSE ONE – Write Contestant NUMBER

BEST DRESS:

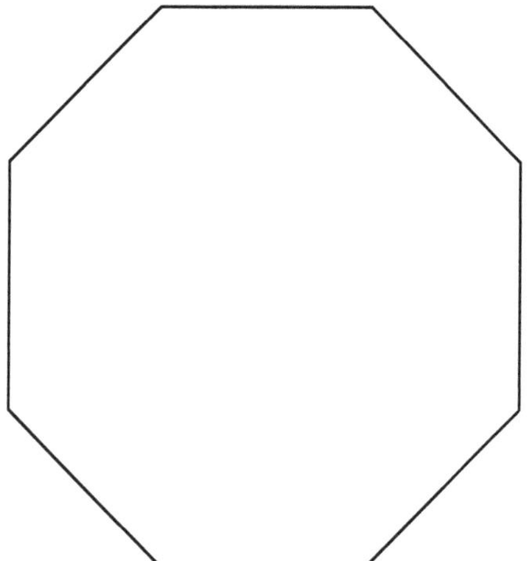

CHOOSE ONE – Write Contestant NUMBER

BEST HAIR

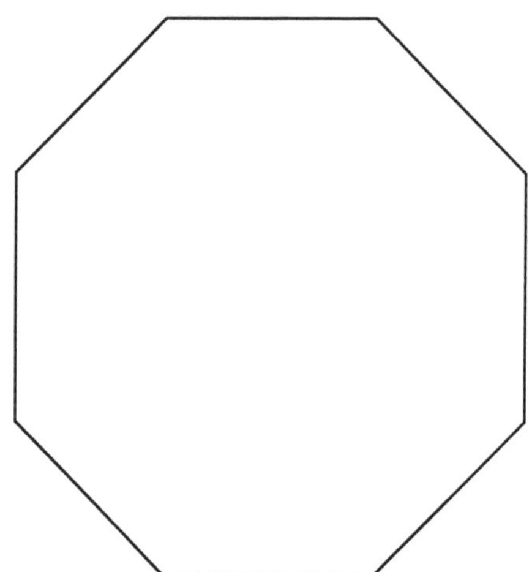

BEAUTY & OPTIONALS SCORESHEET

_________________________ DIVISION

ALL SCORES 1 – 10

ON-STAGE				OPTIONALS				
#	POISE/ Facial Beauty for Babies	STAGE PRESENCE/ PERSONALITY	OVERALL APPEARANCE	PHOTO	DRESS	HAIR	EYES	SMILE
1								
2								
3								
4								
5								
6								
7								
8								
9								
10								
11								
12								
13								
14								
15								

Judge # _____ SIGNATURE: ______________________________________

AUDITOR'S RESULTS SHEETS TO GIVE TO EMCEE

In the ____________________division our optional winners are:

Photogenic: #_____ ________________________

Prettiest Dress: #_____ ______________________

Prettiest Hair: #_____ _______________________

Prettiest Eyes: #_____ _______________________

Prettiest Smile: #_____ ______________________

And our __________________ winner is:
#_____ ____________________________________

Our Second Runner-Up is: [slight pause]
#_____ ____________________________________

Our First Runner-Up is: [slight pause]
#_____ ____________________________________

And our new - ____ Queen is.... [PAUSE FOR DRUMROLL]
#_____ ____________________________________

AUDITOR Initial_______ DIRECTOR Initial_______

JUDGES Initials: _________ ___________ ____________

SAMPLES

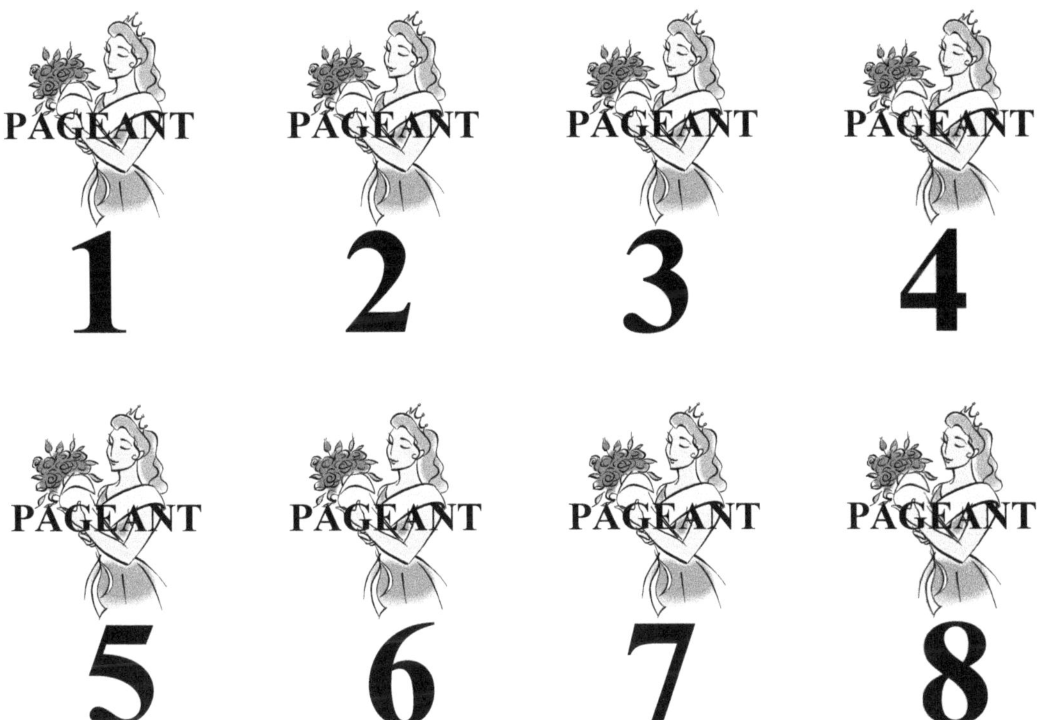

Copy or scan at 200% on card paper

VISITING QUEENS SIGN-IN SHEET

YOUR NAME	YOUR TITLE

Waiver of Liability Form

ALL CONTESTANTS PARENTS MUST SIGN

By signing below I agree to hold harmless all pageant directors and staff; the facility or any employees against any theft or injury in transit to, during or after the pageant. I also agree that the judges decisions are final and acknowledge that bad sportsmanship conduct may cause ejection from the facility and/or request to not attend any more. Cash awards are not guaranteed and no refunds are given unless the event is cancelled.

#	CONTESTANT	SIGNATURE OF PARENT OR GUARDIAN
1		
2		
3		
4		
5		
6		
7		
8		
9		
10		
11		
12		
13		
14		
15		

SAMPLE SCHEDULE:

(Sweetheart – Little):

Welcome
Miss Model Competition:
    Sweetheart
    Princess
Petite
    Little Miss
Introduction of Judges & Auditors
Beauty Competition:
    Sweetheart
    Princess
Petite
    Little Miss
Introduction of Visiting Queens
Entertainment (If Needed) – OR MISS MODEL JR - MS
Awards & Crowning
    People's Choice Queen
    Mini Supreme Ceremony
    Sweetheart – Little Division Queens

(Jr – Ms):

Miss Model Competition:
    Junior Miss
    Teen Miss
    Miss
Beauty Competition:
    Junior Miss
    Teen Miss
Ms
    Miss
Entertainment (If Needed)
Awards & Crowning
    People's Choice Queen
    Grand Supreme
    Junior – Ms Division Queens

SAMPLE SOUND TECH & STAGE MANAGER SCHEDULE

STAGE MANAGER & SOUNDMAN
1:00 Schedule – (Sweetheart – Little):
[PLAY INTRO]
Welcome
[BEGIN FASHION BEATS MUSIC]
Miss Model Competition:
    Sweetheart
    Princess
Petite
    Little Miss
[END FASHION BEATS MUSIC]
[CLOSE CURTAINS]
Introduction of Judges
[OPEN CURTAINS]
Beauty Competition:
    Sweetheart
    Princess
Petite
    Little Miss
Introduction of Visiting Queens
Entertainment (If Needed) [ ]
Awards & Crowning
    People's Choice Queen
    Mini Supreme Finalists (Top 3, 5 or 10)
  Crowning of Mini-Supreme [PLAY FANFARE FOR ANNOUNCING SUPREME]
[LET QUEEN TAKE WALK-GET PHOTOS – THEN CLOSE CURTAINS]
[LINE-UP SWEETHEARTS ON STAGE WITH MOMS – HAVE EVERY OTHER DIVISION LINED UP, OFF STAGE, IN ORDER AND READY TO GO]
    Crown Sweetheart – Little [Play Drumrolls to Announce QUEENS]
[LET QUEENS TAKE WALK FOR PHOTOS AND THEN DISMISS FOR NEXT GROUP]

NOTES

NOTES

NOTES

NOTES

www.ingramcontent.com/pod-product-compliance
Ingram Content Group UK Ltd.
Pitfield, Milton Keynes, MK11 3LW, UK
UKHW051134260726
13967UKWH00010B/3049

9 780557 097197